FRIEDA HUGHES
STONEPICKER

FRIEDA HUGHES was born in London in 1960, and grew up in Devon. She wrote and and painted from an early age. Since studying at St Martin's School of Art, she has shown her paintings in several solo and group exhibitions in Britain, the United States and Australia.

She has published seven children's books, most recently *Three Scary Stories* (HarperCollins, UK, 2001).

Her first collection *Wooroloo* (Bloodaxe, 1999) was a Poetry Book Society Special Commendation. *Stonepicker* (Bloodaxe, 2001) is her second collection.

She lives in London and is married to painter Laszlo Lukacs.

COVER PAINTING:
Stonepicker by Frieda Hughes (2000)

Books by Frieda Hughes

CHILDREN'S BOOKS

Getting Rid of Edna
   (Heinemann, UK; Harper & Row, USA, 1986)
The Meal a Mile (Simon and Schuster, 1989)
Waldorf and the Sleeping Granny (Simon and Schuster, 1990)
The Thing in the Sink (Simon and Schuster, 1992)
Rent-a-Friend (Simon and Schuster, 1994)
The Tall Story (MacDonald Young Books, 1997)
Three Scary Stories (HarperCollins, 2001)

POETRY

Wooroloo
   (HarperCollins, USA, 1998; Bloodaxe Books, UK, 1999;
   Fremantle Arts Centre Press, Australia, 1999)

Stonepicker
   (Bloodaxe Books, UK, 2001; HarperCollins, USA, 2001)
   Fremantle Arts Centre Press, Australia, 2001)

FRIEDA HUGHES

Stonepicker

BLOODAXE BOOKS

ISBN: 1 85224 564 6

First published 2001 by
Bloodaxe Books Ltd,
Highgreen,
Tarset,
Northumberland NE48 1RP.

Bloodaxe Books Ltd acknowledges
the financial assistance of Northern Arts.

Cover printing by J. Thomson Colour Printers Ltd, Glasgow.

Printed in Great Britain by
Cromwell Press Ltd, Trowbridge, Wiltshire.

For Laszlo Lukacs
and in memory
of my father.

ACKNOWLEDGEMENTS

Acknowledgements are due to the editors of the following publications in which some of these poems first appeared: *London Magazine* (for 'My Face', 'Phone Call' and 'The Dying Room) and *The Spectator* ('Landmines'). 'Stonepicker', 'The Signature' and 'The Last Secret' were broadcast on *Midweek* (BBC Radio 4).

CONTENTS

Stonepicker

She is scooped out and bow-like,
As if her string
Has been drawn tight.

But really, she is
Plucking stones from the dirt
For her shoulder-bag.

It is her dead albatross,
Her cross, her choice,
In it lie her weapons.

Each granite sphere
Or sea-worn flint
Has weight against your sin,

You cannot win.
She calls you close,
But not to let you in, only

For a better aim.

Playground

They were practising themselves,
Trying out their little fists.
But a punch was nothing new,
It did not have that resounding shock
Of being just invented.

Big girl shook her short hair.
Hot and wretched,
She was boiled in her skin
As if she must
Unpeel at any moment.

Her blue wool and grey skirt
Were dragged and twisted round
Her fleshy mountains, and
Small girl laughed as
Agile as a goat, and wide-eyed,

Using words that stuck
Like gum on shoes,
Better than a fist and leave a bruise,
And all the legs of little boys
Like bars, and all their noise

Filling up the big girl's head
With memories of ridicule
That would repeat again, again,
For years inside her brain. She knew
One thing must stop it now

Or face it every day at school.
She watched the other girl, mouth wide,
Laugh and point, no matter
How she cried. Her idea was simple;
Take the laugh away.

The small girl didn't scream at first, until
Her bloody lump of thigh
Was bitten out and left.
No more than a mouthful, it silenced laughter
Among the children in the playground

Long after.

Soldier

There are different kinds of war.
In one, a nineteen-year-old girl
Steps aside, in the park,
For a pregnant woman. She slips
On mud and sodden grass.
Arms out for a fall, her wrists crack
Like two pencils, in unison
With an elbow and an ankle.

The ambulance arrives. Her hands
Are gently wiped, to clean
Dog shit from between
Her fingers. Then
Her face is wiped of blood
Where her forehead hit,
And her tears are wiped
With a cloth of blood and shit.

By the time her wrists have healed,
Her eyes are empty. Toxocara
Has crept in, through the cloth of kindness,
Of ignorance, through the skin
Of her corneas. Forty-three operations,
One for a metal heart-beat,
And she is twenty-six today, on a train,
Telling two strangers how

She finds her own dog's shit now,
With the animal's nose, a rubber glove
And a plastic bag. Her words negotiate filth,
As her hands do. A lavatory is where
She cleans each plastic rim
And unseen bit of porcelain,
Just to have a pee. Her mind's eye
As sharp as her nose for a smell.

Her black dog takes two seats.
He's earned it. His rump
Is dented like tin, where
A knife was stuck in
When she was mugged
For her white stick and
A bag of wet-wipes.
It's not as if she had a husband to save her.

He died of cancer last year.
Before him, her five-month-old son
Exhaled a last breath.
His little body invisibly blue
And cold to the touch, in his cot,
In his death. Once, she believed in God.
Now she believes she is being taken
A piece at a time.

All she wants back
Are the birthday flowers from her luggage,
Put on the wrong train
By someone with eyes, who could see.

Visitants

Trees crabbed in their leaves,
Bundled black like old women.
Hunchbacked and planted,
Breathless,
They waited for sound.

Houses, subsiding like three-storey
Headstones in a burial ground,
Were blind to the street.
Their flat eyes and doors
Shut like mouths against noise.

And it came.
Hauling its body of notes
Through the night air,
It came. Dragging its throat behind
Like invisible rope, it came.

When it arrived, fixed as I was
Like a camera, I could picture nothing.
The screech repeated as if
To pick itself out and
Hold itself up for a look, at nothing.

For a year, the study window
Was my waiting eye
For the dying goose, or a cat
Beneath a slowly rolling truck,
Anything that could make that cry.

Until one night, my car
Opened up a mouth beneath its windpipe
And scraped asphalt with that same howl;
A bloody-ended, shrill stretch of raw meat,
And no murder.

Winter-bushed and city-blackened, two foxes
Scrambled from the wheel arch.
Baiting each other like lovers,
They collected their noise.
It untangled between them like a joke.

Stones

These earth-jewels are not dumb.
The diamond ones have life
In a woman's eye, and the black hole

Of a tooth in the mouth
Of a man, with a man's fingers
Fingering his molars. It might

Just make it, if it can quiet
Its bright, compacted soul
In its drill-hole.

And dolerite is the Russian doll
Of the desert. Each cracked egg
Is stripped, a year at a time as

Each boulder exfoliates its onion layers,
Leaving only a large marble that I will
Thread on my necklace.

Their unpeelings rock in the wilderness, each
Wanting to be a cup for water.
And bloody and rough at the roadside

Are the garnets. Like tongue-warts,
Raw, from the mouth of the earth.
Unspoken, they have a whole life

In their little red bodies
If you listen. Not to find a heal
For a wound, or an unpressing

Of a cerebral cortex, or an answer
To a question for the Gods.
Just to hear them.

The Outfit

Long black sat there. Bored on the bones beneath,
Idle over the knees, and flat
Against the back beneath short red.

Short red shifted her sleeves a bit
And cried: 'It wasn't like this, last time!'
Long black sighed. This stillness was wounding.

Last time, neat little weave
That stroked ankles
Had drunk a lot, and tottered.

Black and red had plotted
To take grey wool two-piece to bed,
And succeeded. But tonight, there was nothing doing.

Early at home, they were cupboard-hung
Like little skins. Breathless,
And waiting to be made interesting.

Sisyphus

Dead, she is piled on his back
For the river crossing.

Before, he rolled his stone
Up the mountain while
His wife watched. And then
They watched it roll down again.
It defied him. Now he is
Carrying his wife's carcass.

He reaches the river bank. Mud
Is thick at his ankles.
Her body stinks from
The buckle of his shoulders,
But the gathered crowd
Will not land him. They stand,
Bank-bound, their words
Sharp like swords, and hold him off.

Slowly, current tugging at his
Bent knees, he turns. Slowly,
He wades back. But they are
Waiting there too, tongues pointed
Like knives. And his wife
Is weighing heavy for her burial.

He turns again.

Fear

He sits on the bed-end, my black foot
Foul-mouth friend. Breath like hot bitumen,
His smile is tangled in those rotten teeth,
His hand upon my ankle like a clamp.

He, heavy jailer, holds me for tomorrow
When they cut out the pain,
Take away the lost flesh like the secret body
Of a dead cat wanting burial, and stitch me back again.

I have made him up of my own mud and clay and blood.
I stapled him together. Gave him life.
He is the only one to touch, and sit, and wait with me,
In my dark, in my room, until it's time.

Dr Shipman

God is a doctor. His secret adores him, as close
To his skin as his beard – hedge-cut
To hide all but his letterbox – and his eyes,
Counting down corpses on his abacus
Ten at a time.

The strength in his poisoned needle
Adds inches to him. His power to take,
Or to leave until later,
Must be the joke that splits apart
His foliage to laugh.

Weeping relatives make him
Their Wailing Wall and he watches,
All death certificates and consternation,
From the superior vantage point
Of his mounting body count.

God, undiscovered in his disguise,
Plans his afternoons so death
Is between lunch and dinner,
Like a snack; a little something
That feeds his empty hole.

When God is found out for being
Someone else, he is thrown into jail.
But he still thinks he's God as long
As he holds the answer to the question.
God locks his tongue in a box, and swallows it.

The Wound

She carries her wound,
It is carefully disguised
Beneath her underclothes.
It is still bleeding.

It is her mother's fault,
When her mother imagines
Her child might not be
Blameless.

It is her father's fault,
For not having a hole
Like hers, so
Not understanding.

It is her husband's fault,
For wanting
To stop up her pain
And the pain, stopping.

It is her sister's fault;
Calling her untaught,
When her pain has made her
Very taut indeed.

She lies down with her pain.

It is the sword in the bed
Between her and her lovers,
And her friends and her sister,
Her father and mother.

She sharpens it daily.

Black Cockatoos

The girls are calling.
One with an eye for me,
Rolls in her sky
And lets out a cry
That knots cat hair.
Airborne widows,
Their feathers skip fences.
Under armpit
They bring the bush-heat,
And in their breath
Is the red dirt
Where their wings will fold
When they fall.

The Little War

Victim has turned on killer and
The two of them are arguing
Over a television. Killer took it
When the killing started, but somehow
Victim didn't die,
He came home to find
The contents of his house
Had moved across the street.
Now he wants his television back,
And his fridge, and his
Electric cooker but
No one has pointed out that
The power is down
And the generators are in the hands
Of the Russians again. All he knows is
That his fridge still wears
The alphabet magnets brought home
For his dead son. They hold
The last scrap of his wife's face,
Torn, and left beneath
The letter 'S' and
He is prepared to kill for it.

Communion

Ten years old, she was asleep. Dreaming,
She was dragged from the folds
That clasped her like a ring-stone,

And sat up.

Her head refused to release
The people in it, rolling on her shoulders
With the weight of them.

A face was
Thrust into her face.
An urgent, unlikely face,

Not a house-face.
She must dislodge sleep to see it,
It might never come again.

Her bald eyes struggled for it,
Wanting focus for
A fixing-point.

Ears. He had big ears.
And eyes astonished as her own,
That stared back, unblinking.

Fox met her nose to nose,
So close, his coal-tip was too soon
For a sharp edge.

She wanted to climb inside
His black holes, and stroke
His terror down.

Orphan four-legs, off to find a home,
Brought in to be shown,
Just once.

She was still
Embedded in him as
He was carried to the door.

Incision

He calls her.
Not with his mouth open
And his cracked bead,
But with the two wet lips
Of his surgeon's incision.

As if he had given birth
To his daughter from
His own sliced belly,
And left that mouth open,
Waiting for an answer.

And there she is,
Bearing the same scar.
Tiger stripe for tiger stripe.

In his held breath
Is the nurse with her hand
On the mouthpiece of a phone,
Where his brother sits,
Gagged by her fingers.

Tiger weeps when spear
Parts his second and third ribs,
But understands anyway. Then dies.
Maybe this new mouth
Will have a real shout.

The sound will escape from the stitches
And be heard in the blood
As it dries on the sheets.
A sudden, loud red scream
When the covers are stripped back.

Beauty 1

Picked brows and puckered mouth,
Pumped up with belly fat, and belly
Sucked in through a tube,
Through a hole in you.

The look has become the life. The bed edge
Is pushed further beneath the knife.
A little tuck, a little cut, are not a lot
From last time. Seventh, eighth or ninth time.

But the face is not the one you wore before
Your seventeenth birthday. Men hold it
In their hands, your lips, like petals,
Curling with tattoo. You have made

A thing that only is, if someone looks,
And looks, and looks.

Beauty 2

Italian waiter poured the water
As I waited. The seat opposite
Marking me out as if
I were naked.

I watched the couple
Led to the table beside me.
He had a face that
Thirteen-year-old girls

Would colour-copy twenty times
And pin to their walls, his many eyes
Like swords, polishing on their new breasts. She
Was the surprise. A nothing face.

Not bulbous, nor lumpy,
Nor scarred, nor strange at all. But blank
And plain beneath her mouse-cap of hair.
Hand-held, his looks dwarfed her.

She smiled. There was this
Pulling back of skin to let in light.
Her voice was a pounding river, where he swam
Over the perfect white stones of her teeth.

Her fingers were tiger lilies, dancing.
She was illuminated
Like coloured glass, and he
Was kneeling at her window.

The Bird Cage

It is bright and gold, ring hold
At the top, for a chain.
A little girl is caught in its bars
As surely as the toy bird.

Each of them, perch-bound. One looking out,
The other peering in, but trapped
By those green and blue feathers and
The bead of a dead eye.

Not given to her, she must watch
Another child carry the canary
To a hot spot on the radiator
For its trick.

And there it is left, in the rising air.
The bird shudders as if life has just been
Forced back through its yellow beak
And into its small mechanical breast.

Its wings open, its tail spreads
And suddenly it is singing:
'I should have been yours,
I should have been yours.'

Leaving

On Wednesday, the fridge
And the bed left together
With a woman
In high, black heels.

The table and chairs
Went off with a man
Who came for the TV
And six extension leads.

Hippies in a combi bought the hi-fi,
And the valley turned out
For the garage sale and
A cordless phone.

We were throwing the anchors off!
If someone would only
Steal the car,
We could go.

Phone Call

She's phoning again.
Hardly ever a man would call
This way. Even
A stealer of days would be
More of a javelin thrower.

But her voice is all warm
For the dog in you,
Word-beaten, daring to play again,
With the sucking child
And its rattle of scream.

She opens her mouth,
As big as the door of her house,
To let you in
With your toothpick
For the bits in her teeth,

And the pounding of train
From the back of her tongue,
Through the eye of the telephone.
And when she is done,
She is already calling again.

Warrior

Behind the boy's eyes
Are all the little devils. And you,
You, with your mask over
Everything in front of you,
Want to pound him beneath
The feet you have borrowed.
Picked up with the uniform,
Your boots have pride in being matched
With many others.
They want things. As you
Bring down your cudgel upon
Something you thought would not
Crack that way, all your brothers
Are murdered. And when
You are driven home, driven like
The cattle you killed, like
The people you buried,
There is a man with boots
Towering above, brandishing
His own mace. He is
Reclaiming his place, but now
You are nothing to him either.

Lucky Stone

As near a ball as an eye,
Its dull black as heavy as gold
Was hot in my hand,
I made it my luck.

At a touch all the time,
Pocket polished and as special
As a gift outside birthdays,
It turned in its dark, on its axis.

Stone, by nature, being stone,
Sidled up to the threads that held it.
Smooth though it was, and toothless,
It somehow had teeth.

My hand in my pocket
Found it empty. Suddenly,
Stunned, my brain
Fell to the bucket-bottom.

All my luck had passed
Through a hole. Street-scattered
Among miles of pavement
It was gone.

For days I paced each turn
I'd made, each detour.
Nothing else was as sacred
As my lost luck.

I found a smooth brown pebble
Almost round. A thing that stood out
From the baked dirt.
I slipped it into my pocket.

I was going to find it some friends, but
Nothing would be given my luck again.
It would sit among many, and I
Would give it no importance at all.

Sunset for Ros

At a bonfire
We are fire-watchers. The flames
Dance and dance and dance,
Going nowhere.
We are caught in their red skirts, nonetheless.
Their hot arms embrace us until
Their dance is done,
And they are cold and dead,
And not coming back again.

Sky broadens her grin.
We grow old beneath her.
Ever-returning to begin,
She must watch with a laugh,
Her seams and trenches,
Fresh from the furnace
In which they have rolled and flared,
Come back to burn again. Her light
Picks out our surface, and illuminates
Each new furrow upon
Our waning faces.

She takes our last breath
From the dirt of the day,
And ignites it above deserts,
Where stones look back
At their birth-mother, blazing.

Myra Painting

Myra, Myra on the wall,
Hung at last to please us all.
The little hands that painted you
Thought it a good game
To pick out your face in its frame,
And fill it in with their fingers.

In your own art, your skill is still
Buried with the children. Little unfound bodies,
Stuck inside your casing like you
Nailed down their mothers, hammering them in.
When the passer-by squeezed out the juice
From a fountain pen, theirs was the laugh.

All that is left are mirrors of ink,
Like black pennies, drying
Beneath your vacant lot. Outlined
In a square of white tape, like taping
The fallen body, they are a new installation,
And you have gone to be restored.

Drinker

In the morning
We were friends,
Showing off
Our broken pieces.

We read them like rune stones.
You saw men in mine,
Goldfish in my aquarium, all wanting air
And fighting for freedom.

You saw my canvases unroll
Like open wounds,
And the words of poetry
Spill salt on the bloody parts.

But your stones were heavier;
Their haul of unmade phone calls,
Unbuilt houses, and an ex-wife
With your end in mind, dragged.

Your stones rocked in alcohol, your
Other man bottomed out in your glass
As the food toppled
From your falling plate.

I watched your other person
Leave his head on the table
Like a handbag,
And knew I was too late.

Driver

One day, she will pick this up.
Maybe she will remember
Her silver Volvo station-wagon
And her silent husband and
Her nine-year-old daughter
Crouched in the back seat,
With a boot full of plants and duvets,
And boxes of weekend CDs.

The girl, her face book-open
In the sound of our horn,
As her mother drives
The silver skin of her
Daughter's chariot
At our pale blue.

And me, with my body wondering
Which wounds to wear this time, and she
With her face in the window, loud about
Wanting our place.
She was aiming her bullet
At our noise –
The only thing that caught her
From falling, and she,
Still wanting to drop.

Hospital Waiting Room

Chipped from outback mud
With a pick and mattock,
All his little parts baked together,
His skin of leather
As dug out as gullies.

His broken arm has brought him in
From the oven, his splintered limb
Tied up in the sling of a tea towel. Pain
Pins him to his chair, as if
He has been harpooned in.

The watch upon his wrist
Ticks off its digital seconds.
Hidden in the blue and white check
Of his kitchen cloth, it is
A little bomb waiting to go off.

At three o'clock, we are woken,
Our stupor broken. The screeches
Of his sudden alarm have reached
Into the room's sky,
Pointing him out
Like the arrows of wind vanes.

He suppresses his cry, his tears
Funnel into his hide
Like rain in a creek bed.
This bushman beats desert to squeeze
Water from a branch
And a plastic bag,
But cannot gag the five dollar clock
That straps his broken wing.

His other hand cannot help;
He is thumping the watch
With a cut-off stump and a bit of an elbow,
Three o'clock, three o'clock, three o'clock,
But his melon-end can't make it stop,
And his left hand hangs helpless
Beneath the watch band.

The large woman beside him
Unfolds, her fat forefinger
Leads her eye to the button
That switches him off,
And, for the first time,
His face unbuckles and opens
Just for her.

Landmines

The legs are waiting.
There must be places in Heaven
Where they are stacked fifteen deep,
Along with fingers and arms
From industrial accidents,
All waiting for their bodies to die
And come to find them.

I may meet up with
My womb again,
And a foot of colon that was severed
At its two ends
To become a worm in an Elysian field.

But every day I walk forward
I do not have to know
My legs have gone on ahead.

Mother

Three, like stones, her children lay
Smooth, round and heavy in her lap, her little gods.
Kept her fearful and still, her hair pulled out
Thick by roots, blood made,
When he asked a question.
Wrist skin twisted black,
Each bone a pivot
If she turned her back.

Sharply dragged, her pain was silent
For the heads she cradled.
But his white powder had a loud, hard voice,
Broke those spheres like glass.
Their shattered faces were perfect moons
A moment before his blunt language
Beat out their edges, and he made them
Wrong forever.

The Dying Room

Mother, father, no child,
Made the space between them
Into a hard thing.
A boulder in the bedroom, washed clean
Where they cried. Secretly, and separate.
Each afraid of the other.
Of their invisible baby.
That rock, their burden, should have been a daughter.

And in the dying room, the children gather.
Where death does not need the language,
But picks his nails and cleans his nostrils
With shin bones small enough to knit with.
He knows they will come easily,
Because the cold seek warmth,
And even in his rot and tatters
He wants them most.

Dressed meat, their moons shine.
Tiny girls, not to know
Why brother lived. Never loved,
They grate until they stop,
Little clocks all run out and empty.
They clatter in their graves like hollow tins
And mother, father, no child,
Polish up their stone again.

Crocodiles

Like squeaky toys, their noise
Makes children coo. Their little eyes
Like balls of wide surprise,
Are bugged for mother with
Her mouth of nails. And she,
With limbs like trees
And skin of knotted bark,
And weighing all a ton,
Collects her little ones.
Pouch-rocked in her throat,
She sets them free again
In water, with a tongue
As gentle as fingers.

The Party

They are all out
For the Golden Fleece.
Theseus and Ulysses have found
Carmen Miranda, and hope
They have been recognised.

Hamlet is winding his mother's braid
Around his wrist. Like a watch,
It gives up time.
There is a dark woman
Tapping her fingers on a cold radiator.

She knows who they are. She calculates
Their height and width, she is
Assembling their boxes
And taking photographs,
Until they are all identified.

My Face

As I sleep, other people
Wear my face. It is still
Worn out when I collect it
From the bathroom mirror
In the morning.

I haven't dared a surgeon yet,
To pick off the lines and
Cast adrift the boats
Of my eyes and nose
And mouth.

But in the forty years
That I have seen them all afloat,
Without a cord or chain
To anchor them between my ears,
Above my chin and throat,

My skin spiders and flesh-mites
Have been knitting up each
Facial twitch and scratch. They even caught
The creases from my first laugh,
When I spilled out of the womb.

Longest worked on, it must
Run the deepest. A straight rope
From voice-box to navel. And if the line
Is taut enough, you will hear
It still plays the same note.

Oracle

Only a hole in the wall,
Where fingers have polished
The sill of the voice that speaks
From the gut of your boulder,
And begged for an answer.

The answer stands there, bald
And featherless, on your bottom lip.
It is not always beautiful.
It does not look the way
They think it should.

It opens up the mouth in its
Fleshy mass, in the door of
Your mouth, and the answer
Screeches.
Man bends for his first stone.

Man, Starving

The Saturday supplement had been stacked
And left. No one
Would pick it up and place
That man's face beneath their arm.

His black eyes rattled at the back
Of his deep burrows. Their whites
Were wounds in the newsprint.
They leapt up and got you.

He was four-legged like a dog,
Not from having lost something;
His bones would snap
If he tried to upright his sticks.

His skull smiled up through skin,
Full lips of flesh
Had shrivelled and dried like worms,
His teeth were constantly naked.

And the cameraman, without words,
Had picked him up in his lens
And printed him out, over and over again.
We could almost hear him weeping.

Lunch

You sharpen me like a pencil,
Lighting matches just to burn them out.
Hiding your mud feet beneath the table,
You watch the children die in my face.
I see your hair is greyer now,
I have missed pieces of you.
Remember not to show your holes
Or I am ferret in your earth.
But now I see your face is cleared like water,
Filtered through the stones you give
For me to throw and make
The circles on your surface.
We collect our lost parts.
Between us, they polish like opals.

The Lady M

Her gold is gone now. Gotten old,
She has fallen in on her hard white cage.
Bone-dangled and clattering,

Her face is cut sideways and smiles.
She is my mother-eater, she has cheated me of love.
Dry as a split gourd

She meets me like a relative, a lover even.
But her face has drawn its pale curtains on
The pits that bog it, and

Her eyes are closed.
Their black coals are only painted on
Her hollow doll. She herself has gone.

Jezebel

She must imprint him,
She is screaming at the door
To be let in.

One time, she must have him.
Maybe twice, to tattoo his elements
To her uneventful skin.

His stain on the folds of her membrane,
Her Turin shroud,
Could lose him his name.

Added to the others,
He will flesh her out. She is nothing
Except through her lovers.

Is he ever going to let her in?

* * *

Down on her luck,
Jezebel is counting her conquests.
Unknown to them
They have fallen.
She is thinking of selling them off.

She combs her hair and
Applies rouge. Some of them
Are women.

* * *

Jezebel's head
Had been severed
By a cart wheel. It rolls off,
Followed by dogs and children.

Her body will pack
Into a small bag,
Every broken bone
Another hinge.

'Am I not beautiful?' she cries,
Her last sentence whispered
From her blunt neck-end
Like the whistle of a hollow reed.

A passing woman bends over the open mouth
And fills it with dirt.
'Quiet, now,' she says,
'Or someone will hear you.'

Endometriosis

It crawls up through the groin.
Nail hooks pick out steps in soft red,
Seeking places to implant
Like a cat, screaming and curious,
Trapped, too fat with feeding
To get out through the way in.

It takes root and flowers, its bloody petals
Falling where no wind blows to rid the earth-flesh
Of the shedding velvet, that clogs and gags.
The claw-roots run too deep to peel
From the hollows of the inside,
It must be made hungry to die.

The only answer is to steal its food bowl,
And cut out the unborn children.

Laugh

Pack animals
Make their food funny.
Hunger hesitates. They watch
What is left on the leg
Still walk, wearing its open wounds.

What hangs from the shoulder
Is a shorter skin, teats
Or testicles dangling, bald,
And bare to air. Bloodied, even,
But left as bobbing ornaments. And there,

Heaving with mateship, nursing
Swollen bellies from another meal,
The beasts lie grassed and steaming.
They watch their food perform
The little dance it does,

Gathering up its fleshy pieces
Like torn petticoats,
To take its stumble and cakefoot
And leave their table, wanting time
To heal.

The Writer's Leg

His body parts knew better
What his talent was. Contentedly, they stretched,
Grew, and waited, growing hairs.

But he was a boy then, and the blood
That pumped him like a piston never let him sit
Long enough to find it.

His arms and legs drew lots to see
Which one would win the right
To let him know and make him listen.

'Not me!' his right arm cried, 'he needs me
For his very purpose. My fingers dance,
Their music is the thing we fight for.'

'Nor me!' his left arm cried. 'As you can see,
I am the balance for all those computer keys.
Without my digits, he does not add up!'

The legs met each other at the knee,
And conferred. They decided on skates.
The first to give in, fall off, or buckle

Would find itself free
To make this boy listen to his head
Above the sound of his own feet, running.

The blind car drove backwards
And hit him hard, so he noticed.
Left him lying there, broken.

His left leg apologised from its
Stitched skin and splinters
For not giving the right leg a proper chance.

Fresh and bloody from its third operation,
Its mouths grinned up at the head and said;
'Now sit and write something.

Where others use a pencil,
You have me. I am your gift.
So use me wisely.'

The San Francisco Fire

The Forty Niners played the fire
At the Candlestick Stadium.

The men were on the field
When the plane flew over,
Tail trailing flag advertising a sale.
And the oval skylight was shut as if
Night had clamped it.

So many people with radios
Now switched them on. Watched
The game at the same time
They heard the flames on interview.
Eucalyptus burns best, and the hotel exploded.

The commentary took trees down, ten at a time.
Someone scored a touchdown,
And we knew the people leaving
Were homeless already.
Then came the slow, black snow

With their furniture in it.
And their toys and their photographs,
The water from their swimming pools
And everything in the garden shed.
The crowd cheered. The fire won.

And we walked to our cars in our hundreds,
With the black dust of burned homes
Thick on our chests and shoulders,
In our hair and on our forearms.
We carried the shadow as one.

Salmon

The boy stood, adolescent,
In the river gravel, holding
His dead salmon. Its eyes
Begged up at him, with clouds in them,
And his own eye.

By degrees, he sank. His ankles
Were disappearing and still
The fish lay cold in his palms.
The gravel pebbled against his
Soft, white man-flesh, and in it
Rolled a hundred nested embryos
And he, still clutching the father,
The carcass.

Portrait

Blind, she is painted empty.
Her hollow vessel clatters like a seedpod,
Wanting water and a stem to see with.

On the still beach of her face
All her creatures are stuck
In the oil of her shoreline.

Beneath the rocks of her shoulders
Are the mountainous happenings
That moulded her.

And in her voice, lies her landscape,
Pitted with caves
Of secret wishes for sight,

Beneath the trees of her fingers
Whose roots touch everything,
Bringing everything back

To her black holes.
Had she been put to music,
We would have seen her.

Beetle

The little beetle curls his mouse
Into a basket. Tucking in paws,
And tying in the tail.

The mouse is amenable
By way of being dead
From a beetle-bite.

The beetle burrows into
The soft centre of mouse-belly,
And lays out her embryos like jewels.

Squirming with the separation of cells,
They grow, split and feed, on their casket,
Becoming maggots.

They hollow out their bloody stink-nest
Of dead flesh, which still wears
Its mouse face,

Fattening to fall, and become beetles again.
The first ones out
Get to eat their brothers and sisters.

The Other Amy

She has a secret.

She has nursed it for years.
It has grown up inside her
Like a tree, each branch
Fingered into her blood vessels
As if feeding her,
But she feeds it.

Every morning,
Like a dependant plant,
It receives water.
Every morning
She repeats to it
Her thoughts.

Quietly, she has been
Building her root map for years,
A finger's inch at a time.
If only they knew,
It would shut their open faces
Like doors.

Left Luggage

He was born like a box,
Put together with sides
Of mother and father and
Everyone trying to read
The label of contents.

For a long time, he looked after
Each of his occasions, even
That moment when his wife left him.
It was hung from a hook
On one of his walls.

He used to stand inside himself
Sometimes, and have a look.
Dangling in his gallery, it rather
Overshadowed his smaller memory of
Their meeting at the fishmongers.

Between their beginning and end
Was a Nepalese mountain,
The heal for a scar from a straw-jump;
A hidden spike,
And drinks at six weddings.

It was easier just to smell fish,
And forget her.
Even his brother's first bike
That he stole, was parked
Up against the punishment.

The day came when all the weight
Of a Sumo was accommodated in his frame.
He no longer rattled with expectation.
His digestion was slow and his belly dragged,
Something must be shed, to move him on.

His internal shelf was weighted down
By his book of self,
Everything was written in.
For weeks, he fingered his
Own pages, trying to work out

What to lose and what to keep,
And what to look at longer.
He read himself over.
Finally, when he had remembered everything,
He got up for a cup of coffee.

Leaving all his chapters
On a park bench,
He realised that
He didn't have to go
Back for them.

Silence

If I am silent for long,
Maybe twenty minutes, you will
Fill that quiet with the sound
Of your own traffic, a dog bark,
And the voices of all the people
That inhabit your mind and
Make up your memory;

Your several brothers and sisters
Sitting in an elm tree,
The branches cracking beneath their
Gathered weight like hot fat,
The two wash-hanging mothers
Tossing their words like sock-balls,
To and fro, across the fences at the back,
And the first and last partners
You ever made love with.

By the time I speak again,
You may no longer believe me.

If I am silent for years,
You may even bear my children,
Marry my husbands and mourn
The death of my parents. You could
Chop trees from my hillside,
Imagine the smell of my lilies, and complain
My shoes do not consider your feet at all.

If I never speak,
You could invent me completely.

Bagman

The cloth is torn
And stripped, and laid
Like splints along his legs.
Tied with string
To keep him in,

He is heaped. A sack
Of spilling clothes, all rubbished,
That rise and fall with sleep.
And in the rain, his fraying ends
Struggle to escape their knots and twists,
The man inside his chrysalis.

The Secret

She was desperate to know,
And I so longed to tell her.
The words rolled in my mouth
Like sour little beads. Lemon seeds,
Waiting for the spike of her needle to find
The holes in them, and my tongue.

A right word would unwrap
The secret like a bloody gift,
Bought over someone else's body.
I didn't give it. But it was
Pointed out by all my efforts
Not to tell.

Will she, who understands,
Become now dangerous?
Or is she after all,
A proper keeper of
My sullen jewel?

Breasts

Scarred beneath their bags
Of heavy silicone,
They were mountains,
Shored up and sharpened,
A handful of the mind's mud
At a time. Those breasts

Weren't for a limp sweater,
Or a bra size more than
Two saucers. Those breasts
Had purpose. Men's eyes
Would unpage magazines
For a sight of them.

Melissa was no longer
Required to speak.
Her breasts could talk.
They had a language
And everyone
Understood.

When at last she made the photo shoot,
She gently placed her breasts
Of shiny plastic flesh
Upon the table for
The cameraman,
And left.

Foxhead

Stunned, it was listening
To two men talk. Goggling,
Its eyes, glass-beaded, popped,
And its ears were pricked
For every word. Like a telephone

Pretending it could hear,
The cord-end
Severed,
This head's neck
Wasn't going anywhere.

The Signature

One for you, one for me,
The books are being
Divided between us. Leftovers
From a library where, at night
In the dark, or between
Dinner downstairs and the bathroom,
Sticky fingers would find
Whole volumes stuck to them.

Each book is opened, and there
She has written her name. A mother
For you, a mother for me,
Another for you, another for me,
And suddenly, a small square
Cut from the page corner where
Her ink had dried.

Perhaps the coat pocket was
Too small for the whole story,
But just big enough
For the nail scissors.

For Ted and Leonard

The bird was broken.
Cracked open. Split like a pod.
From inside its Siamese halves
Its two fathers looked up
At the sky they had made,
And the creatures that had crawled
Out of the pit of each
Sibling mind and lived,
Breathing, with heartbeat,
Even as their own failed.

Each pulsed like a lung
In his half-shell,
Blowing the beak like a horn
To make it speak; their shared mouth
Until one ceased. The other, listened
In disbelief. Waiting, waiting, waiting
For the next word, using his one claw
To draw, mostly himself, as if
The dead half would suddenly
Return to write the narrative,
With stickled fingers pushed into
The other bird-claw glove, pen-held
And laughing at his joke. Instead,
In silence, nothing happened.

The half-bird, still attached
To his memory of being whole,
Found it harder and harder
To think about anything
Except finding his lost part.
So at last, he left
To go looking.

Crow rocked in the dirt, in the wind,
Blameless at last.

The Last Secret

Is the elephant in the room.
We can't speak about it, even though
It stalks you. Thorny-haired,
Its eyes of nostril turning always to you,
As if you have some special smell.

It stalks us next, but for now
It wants you first.
You don't want its word
Anywhere, or in our mouths.
Its presence makes us dumb.

So, it is the elephant in the room.
In my sleep, I take a gun
And shoot it dead. But in the morning
Its weight is at our feet again,
Wanting to be fed.

Its body is on the hearthrug
More faithful than any dog,
And beside the table, and
Beside you in the car, even though
I sit there; its mournful, stupid eyes

Unable to avoid you. Slowly,
Its breath is stealing your breath,
Its heavy feet rest upon
The altar of your chest. Tonight
I am going to kill it again.

Conversation with Death

Death has come to have a look
At his work.
Sitting by my father's coffin, fingers
Linked in his lap like any doctor,
He is smiling.

'You took him too soon,'
I say.

'It wasn't easy,' he tells me. 'Every time
I found a way to get him,
He slipped out of it.
That first time, I was sure
The cells I chose would do it.
I watered each blessed seed.
I visited daily. My flowers flowered,
But I found he could uproot them
With almost a thought. Each day
Was stolen from me. Even when
I had him by the heart;
Tried to stop it beating,
Held it fast with my two hands, it was as if
He climbed inside his own crawl space
And picked off my fingers, one by one.

'You could have left him longer,'
I protested.

Death frowned. 'To take some
Poor soul, car-crashed by the roadside,

Or with bullet holes and
A leg blown off, is easy.
There is no grace in that.

'But to take a Greatness, who fights
With all that accumulated excellence,
Derived from a full time, even
Had in a short time,
Is an art.

'I could have had him in his thirties,
I wanted him then.
I have wanted him all along.
If I told you I nearly
Lifted him off a train when he
Was only forty-two or forty-three, and a
Little arrhythmia was going to be
My percussion's end
To his ebb and flow of corpuscles,
Could you not see
How lucky you are
To have had him for longer?

'I let him ripen on his tree
Like a heavy fruit. But to wait
Until his stalk broke, in his eighties
Or maybe even his nineties, to have him
Roll into my lap like a ripe fig,
Would have ruined me.

'To take him at the peak of his
Perfection, when he was at his
Escaping most cleverest, meant
I really got to achieve something.'